Helping Children See Jesus

ISBN: 978-1-64104-071-6

Eternity
The Lord Reigns Forever
New Testament Volume 45: Revelation Part 4

Author: Ruth B. Greiner
Illustrator: Vernon Henkel
Computer Graphic Artist: Ed Olson
Typesetting and Layout: Patricia Pope

© 2018 Bible Visuals International
PO Box 153, Akron, PA 17501-0153
Phone: (717) 859-1131
www.biblevisuals.org

All rights reserved. No part of this publication may be reproduced, stored in a retrieval system or transmitted in any form by any means, electronic, mechanical, photocopy, recording or otherwise, without the prior permission of the publisher, except as provided by USA copyright law.

RELATED ITEMS

To access related items (such as activities, memory verse posters and translated texts) please visit our webstore at www.biblevisuals.org and enter 1045 in the search box on the page.

FREE TEXT DOWNLOAD

To access a FREE printable copy of the teaching text (PDF format) in English or other available languages, enter S1045DL in the search box. Add the item to your cart, and use coupon code XTACSV17 at checkout. Once your order is processed you will receive an email with a link to the free download.

STUDENT ACTIVITES

These are included with the FREE printable copy of the English teaching text for this story. See the directions under Free Text Download (above) to access them.

Alleluia: for the Lord God omnipotent reigneth. Let us be glad and rejoice, and give honor to Him.

Revelation 19:6b-7a

© Bible Visuals International Inc

Lesson 1
THE MARRIAGE IN HEAVEN AND THE WAR ON EARTH

NOTE TO THE TEACHER

This is a chapter of contrasts–the blessed marriage and supper of the Lamb contrasted with Christ's frightful judgment on God's enemies at Armageddon. Why must there be an Armageddon? Dr. Charles Ryrie of our Editorial Board, gives three important reasons:

1. **God must punish.** In grace, God has put up with our backsliding. But the time will come when God must punish rebels.
2. **Israel is 'the apple of His eye'** (Zechariah 2:8). God must vindicate His people. Israeli armies commit evil. It does not mean that whatever Israelis do today is right. Our interest must be in the people and in their souls.
3. **Mankind must come to the feet of the King of kings.**

PLEASE NOTE!

To review the future program of God, see the chart on page 28. Using the illustrations in Volume 44, have students mention the coming events. Write them on a chalkboard, so all can copy the chart in their notebooks.

The lessons in this volume are packed with material. Therefore you may want to make two or more lessons out of each one.

Scripture to be studied: Revelation 19

The *aim* of the lesson: To show that nothing will stop the plan and purpose of God.

What your students should *know*: That every true believer in Christ is included in God's glorious plan.

What your saved students should *feel*: A desire to do good deeds so they will be beautifully clothed at "the marriage of the Lamb."

What your saved students should *do*: Determine how they can fill their lives with righteous deeds.

Lesson outline (for the teacher's and students' notebooks):

1. The Alleluia Chorus (Revelation 19:1-6).
2. The marriage and supper of the Lamb (Revelation 19:7-10).
3. The King returns (Revelation 19:11-16).
4. Christ judges evil armies at Armageddon (Revelation 19:17-21).

The verses to be memorized:

Alleluia: for the Lord God omnipotent reigneth. Let us be glad and rejoice and give honor to Him.
(Revelation 19:6b, 7a)

THE LESSON

Voices! Voices! Voices! Many different kinds of sounds can come from voices. Each sound can have a different meaning. Can you think of some sounds and their meanings? A scream might mean someone is frightened. A cry shows that a person needs help. A sob may be a sign of great sorrow. A shout could tell of something important. A laugh usually means the person is happy.

In today's lesson we shall learn about the sound of many voices which John, the apostle, heard more than two thousand years ago. Whose voices did he hear? They were joyous and glorious. Why such gladness?

For thousands of years people on earth have been praying to God: "Let Your kingdom come." "Rule over the earth." "Please stop the evil in the world." And God has promised to put all enemies under His feet. (See 1 Corinthians 15:25.)

1. THE ALLELUIA CHORUS
Revelation 19:1-6

Show Illustration #1

God showed John that a day will come when He will put down all His enemies. The prayers of the saints will be answered. And the people will shout and praise God saying, "Alleluia" [meaning praise ye the Lord]. In the future day they will continue to sing: "Salvation and glory and honor and power unto the Lord our God, for true and righteous are His judgments." God has promised to judge all evil and He will do so. His promise is true. He is righteous, so He always does right–though sometimes He waits long before answering the prayers of His people.

Again the great chorus in Heaven will call out: "Alleluia."

The voices will join together in holy worship. And the twenty-four (24) elders and the living creatures will fall down and worship God who will be sitting on His throne. (See Revelation 4:4; 6b through 9–read text in lessons 2 and 3 of Volume 43.) They too will join in saying, "Amen [that is, so be it]; Alleluia [praise the Lord]. For the Lord God omnipotent [all-powerful] reigns. [He is King.] Let us be glad and rejoice and give honor to Him for the time has come for the marriage of the Lamb. And His wife has made herself ready."

These happy people will be praising God for His victory over His enemies–including Babylon, the false church (Revelation 19:2; compare Revelation 17:1). They will also praise Him for the greatest wedding of all times–the marriage of the Lamb.

2. THE MARRIAGE AND SUPPER OF THE LAMB
Revelation 19:7-10

Show Illustration #2

Who will be the Bridegroom in this future marriage? Who will be the bride? Who will attend the wedding?

The Bridegroom is the Lamb of God, the Lord Jesus. He is the One who many years ago came to earth to give His life for sinners. He is the One who arose from the dead on the third day after dying on the cross. Later He returned to Heaven, promising to come back in the clouds for those on earth who trusted in Him. He will keep that promise. Then the saints will be with Him in Heaven. And He, the Lamb of God, will be the Bridegroom in the most important wedding in the universe.

But what about the bride? Who will she be? The bride will be the saints–the true Church of the Lord Jesus Christ.

– 19 –

The wedding cannot take place until after the false church is judged. (See Revelation 17-18.) After the false church will be judged, the true Church (which includes every genuine believer in Jesus Christ as Saviour) will be ready to become the bride of the Lamb of God. (See Ephesians 5:22-27.)

In a wedding on earth, everyone likes to see the special dress the bride wears. In the heavenly wedding, the bride will be dressed in clean and white fine linen. This special gown has an important meaning. On earth the bride had been clothed in the robe of righteousness (the righteousness of God). All believers receive this robe when they put their trust in Christ as Saviour. Through faith in Him, a person becomes part of the bride of Christ because of His righteousness. (See Ephesians 2:8-9; Titus 3:5; Isaiah 61:10.)

But on this special day which is coming, the bride will wear a gown made of her righteous deeds. Those good deeds done on earth will not help her to get into Heaven. They will not help her to become a part of the bride of Christ. But they will show what she did during her life since she first belonged to Christ. Her service on earth will have been done for God's glory through the help and power of the Holy Spirit. So she will not be proud of herself. Instead, she will give praise to God alone who helped her to do what was right and pleasing to Him. What pleasure this will bring to the Bridegroom!

After the glorious wedding, there will be a celebration. John was told to write down these words: "Blessed [happy] are the ones who are called to the marriage supper of the Lamb."

Who will be invited to attend this joyous celebration? They will be the friends of the Bridegroom. (See John 3:29.) These guests will not be the bride. They will be the redeemed of Old Testament times and the believers who will die during the seven years of Tribulation on earth. They will share in this heavenly glory, though they won't be part of the Church. (The Church began at Pentecost and will be caught up from the earth at the Rapture.)

What a happy day for the Bridegroom! What a happy day for the bride! And what a happy day for the guests!

That long-ago day when God showed the future to John, an angel said to him, "These are the true sayings of God." All that John saw and heard will actually take place in the future. John was so overcome that he fell down to worship the angel. Quickly the angel stopped him. "Do not do that!" the angel commanded. "I am your fellow-servant and the servant of your brothers. Worship God. For the testimony of Jesus is the spirit of prophecy." John understood from this that all of prophecy (things to come) really tells something about Jesus. So God, not angels, should be worshiped.

3. THE KING RETURNS
Revelation 19:11-16

Show Illustration #3

After the preview of the wedding and marriage supper, John saw Heaven open up. Some future day a white horse will ride out of Heaven. Riding on the horse will be One who is called Faithful and True. In righteousness He will judge and fight His battles. Who will this One be? Who is the faithful, true One who judges in the right way all the time? He is the Lord Jesus Christ. He is faithful and true to all His promises. All those who now come to Him and believe on Him become part of His Church. He turns no one away today. However, many do not accept His invitation and they turn away from the only One who can give everlasting life.

The time is coming when Jesus Christ, the faithful, true One, will judge the world. The first time He came to earth, He came to save. But the next time it will be different. The eyes of Jesus Christ will look like flames of fire–the fire of judgment. On His head will be many crowns. So we understand that in majesty Christ will come to conquer and to claim His right to be King over the entire earth.

Christ's robe will have blood stains on it. From His mouth will come a sharp sword–the Word of God–His only weapon. All will be able to see His name: "KING OF KINGS AND LORD OF LORDS."

Then John saw that Jesus Christ, the Rider on the white horse, will not be alone in that future day. He will be followed by a large army riding on white horses. Each member of His army will be clothed in fine white, clean linen. Can you guess who they will be? They will be His saints–those who have genuinely placed their trust in Him. His army will be with Him, for He has promised that His own will always be with Him–and He with them. What a sight! A huge army on white horses coming through the air!

4. CHRIST JUDGES EVIL ARMIES AT ARMAGEDDON
Revelation 19:17-21

Show Illustration #4

John saw that the Beast (the man who is against Christ–anti-Christ) and the False Prophet will come to fight against Christ's army (at Armageddon, see Revelation 16:16; see also chapter 13 and lesson 3 of Volume 44). With them will be the kings of earth and their armies made up of millions who will worship the Beast. The great army from Heaven will come closer and closer. The angry army of Satan will be ready to use all its power to fight against God. Who will win?

Amazingly, not one in the great heavenly army will fight. Not one will be hurt. Their Captain, the King of kings, will win over Satan and all the enemy. In that coming day, God's own will watch and see their King conquer all the nations of earth and become the true Ruler over all. The earthly army of Satan will be defeated. The Beast will be captured. The False Prophet who will do miracles and deceive the people (who had on them the mark of the Beast), will be captured. Then he will not be able to protect himself from God. No miracle will save him. The Beast and the False Prophet will be thrown alive into the lake of fire burning with sulphur. The rest of the evil armies also will be overcome by the Rider of the white horse. He indeed will be King of kings and Lord of lords!

After Christ destroys the evil armies, the earth will have to be cleaned up. Huge birds, as commanded by an angel, will fly down to eat the dead bodies. The Lord will have won over Satan and evil.

In that future day, on whose side will you be? Will you be part of the wicked army of Satan? Or will you ride triumphantly with the Lord Christ? If you are His, are you doing good deeds? If so, you will be beautifully clothed in Heaven.

Maybe you are one who has not received the Lord Jesus into your heart. He is God's love gift to you. God knows how awful it is for a person to be separated from Him forever. So He gave Christ, His own dear Son, to take the punishment of your sin. Maybe you think you're only ignoring Christ–not rejecting Him.

*You have been told that Christ's salvation is a free gift. It is something like offering you this dollar bill. (*Teacher*: Show a piece of money which is familiar to your people.)

Here it is. It is free. All you have to do is take it. There are several ways you can refuse to take it. You can deliberately get up and walk away. By that action you show, beyond any doubt, that you do not wish to have this money. You can come up here and tell me plainly that you do not want my money. Both of these actions would be outright rejections of my offer. But there is another way you can refuse my gift. You can just sit there and ignore me. You do not have to leave or say one word to me. All you have to do is nothing. And you are refusing my offer. You see, ignoring my gift amounts to the same as rejecting it.

Maybe that is what you have been doing about the Lord Jesus Christ. You are not openly rejecting Him. You are simply ignoring Him. There are different ways to refuse God's salvation. But there is only one way to get it. That is to receive the Saviour into your own heart. If you would like to do that today, will you bow your head now and ask the Lord Jesus to come into your heart and save you? Ignoring Him means rejection. Receiving Him means salvation.

* From *Easy Object Lessons* by Dr. Charles C. Ryrie. Published by Moody Press, Chicago, IL, 60610. Copyright 1970. Used by permission.

NOTE TO THE TEACHER

If you feel that there is more in this lesson than your pupils can understand, divide it and make two lessons.

If you teach with conviction, your students will know that you yourself believe that the One of whom you speak is indeed the living and true God.

It is suggested that in their notebooks (which all members of your class should have) they should write the four main points of the lesson. Or, if they prefer, have them make four simple drawings like those on illustration #4. This will help them to remember the lesson.

Lesson 2
SATAN DEFEATED–CHRIST VICTORIOUS

NOTE TO THE TEACHER

One of the most important laws of teaching is:

Review, review, review.

This is especially necessary when teaching the truths of the Word of God. Much–perhaps all–that is in these lessons is new to your pupils. It is not enough simply to *tell* the lessons. The learners must understand what you are teaching. Remember that you are not teaching *lessons*; you are teaching *people*. Give them opportunities to ask questions. If there is more here than can be understood in one lesson, divide it into two lessons. May the Book and its glorious message live to you, dear teacher! Then it will live to your pupils.

Keep this verse before your class:

Ye turned to God from idols to serve the living and true God. (1 Thessalonians 1:9)

Scripture to be studied: Revelation 20

The *aim* of the lesson: To show the final judgment of Satan and all who follow him.

What your students should *know*: That a perfect earth–even without temptations of Satan–will not change sinful hearts.

What your students should *feel*: A dread of having any of their family, friends, or anyone, punished forever and separated from God for all eternity.

What your students should *do*: Pray for those who do not know Christ, witness faithfully, seek to live so others will yearn to come to Christ.

Lesson outline (for the teacher's and students' notebooks):
1. Satan imprisoned (Revelation 20:1-3).
2. The one thousand-year reign (The Millennium) (Revelation 20:4-6).
3. Satan's rebellion and doom (Revelation 20:7-10).
4. The Great White Throne Judgment (Revelation 20:11-15).

The verses to be memorized:

Alleluia: for the Lord God omnipotent reigneth. Let us be glad and rejoice and give honor to Him.

(Revelation 19:6b, 7a)

THE LESSON

Have you ever heard someone say, "The devil made me do it"? Suppose a mighty creature could catch the devil and chain him in a faraway prison. Would everybody on earth do only right? In our lesson today we are going to learn something interesting which answers this question.

The Apostle John, as old as he was, must have had good eyesight! Again and again in the book of Revelation he tells of things he *saw*. He did not seem to miss anything. And best of all, he wrote down what he saw. Now, by studying Revelation, we can learn about all the amazing future which God has planned. Many millions of people, however, are missing these prophecies because they will not read them in God's Book.

1. SATAN IMPRISONED
Revelation 20:1-3

Every believer should know what John saw next. For all he saw will certainly take place. Some future day a mighty angel will come down from Heaven. In his hands he will carry a key and a great chain. The key is to open the abyss (a deep, unmeasurable pit). And the chain? The angel will be sent to capture the devil (also called Satan, the Dragon, that Old Serpent).

> **NOTE TO THE TEACHER**
> The first coming of the Lord Jesus Christ to earth was foretold many times in the Old Testament. This included His birth, His life, His suffering, His death and resurrection. Yet Bible scholars tell us that His coming again and the setting up of His Kingdom on earth are referred to in the Old Testament at least four times more often than His first coming. (Some say 24 times more often!) When He comes as King, He will clear the earth of all rebellion. Use a cup of sand for the concluding object lesson.

Show Illustration #5

The heavenly angel will catch Satan and bind him with the chain. Only God can make a chain strong enough to hold Satan. And God will give that angel the power to fasten the devil. The angel will then unlock the abyss with the key. He will hurl man's worst enemy, Satan, into that great pit and lock him in. God's angel will seal the pit so the devil will not be able to get out. There Satan will be locked up–not for only a day, or a month, but for 1,000 years!

What a victory that will be! No longer will Satan rule. No longer will he deceive people on earth.

Think about it–one thousand years on earth without the devil! Remember, this will take place (1) *after* the Rapture when Jesus Christ comes in the clouds to take all true believers to Heaven; (2) *after* the seven years of tribulation; (3) *after* Jesus Christ comes back to earth as King; and (4) *after* Christ's judgment on the evil armies at Armageddon. It is then that the devil will be chained in the abyss and the one thousand years of peace will begin.

2. THE ONE THOUSAND-YEAR REIGN (THE MILLENNIUM)
Revelation 20:4-6

The thousand years of peace on earth are spoken of as the Millennium. *Millennium* means "one thousand years." Things will be entirely different during the Millennium. The Lord Jesus Christ will be King over the entire earth. This will be a world of peace where even the wild animals will be tame. (See Isaiah 11:1-10; 65:18-25.) Lions will not hurt people. Scorpions and bees will not sting. Wolves and lambs will live together happily. Leopards and baby goats will be good friends. Little calves and young lions will be led by children. Cows and bears will eat their food together without fighting. Even when babies put their hands into the holes, the snakes there will not bite them.

The whole earth will be a safe place in which to live. It will be safe in the cities and safe in the woods. (See Ezekiel 34:25-31.) Fruit, vegetable and flower gardens will grow without weeds, thorns, or thistles. (See Isaiah 55:13.) The desert will blossom as a rose. (See Isaiah 35:1.)

This will then be a world without war, for Jesus Christ, the Prince of Peace, will be the world Ruler. The capital city of the world will be Jerusalem.

Show Illustration #6

When King Jesus Christ reigns over the earth, He will have others ruling with Him exactly as He promised. (See 1 Corinthians 6:2; Revelation 3:21; 5:9-10.) People will live much longer than they do now. Some will live to be hundreds of years old, even a thousand years old, for the curse (of Genesis 3) will be removed. (See Romans 8:18-23.)

During the Millennium some will sit on thrones. These will have lived on earth during the Tribulation. But they did not worship the Beast nor the image. They had refused to receive the mark of the evil Beast on their foreheads or on their hands. They had witnessed for Christ through those awful days of Tribulation. And, rather than turn against God and Christ, they will be beheaded. But during the glorious Millennium, they will be alive again, sitting on thrones and reigning with Jesus Christ for 1,000 years.

Not only martyrs, but others too will rule with Christ. He has promised that those who have been faithful in living for Him and suffering for Him on earth will also rule with Him. (See 2 Timothy 2:12.)

Have you suffered for telling others of Christ? Be glad. You will someday rule with Christ. Maybe you are suffering now. Do not be discouraged nor unhappy. The Apostle Paul said that "the suffering of this present time cannot be compared with the glory which shall be revealed in us" (Romans 8:18). You will be repaid beyond anything you could ever dream.

3. SATAN'S REBELLION AND DOOM
Revelation 20:7-10

At the end of the thousand years, Satan will be unchained and let out of prison. Will he have changed? Will he then do good instead of evil? No, indeed. As soon as he is released, Satan will again lie to people and trick them. Those born during the thousand years who have not repented will be attacked by Satan. He will never change. He will be evil forever. He will gather people from around the world to fight a war against the saints of God and against Jerusalem.

Why will the people on earth listen to Satan? They will have seen the wonderful, peaceful earth under the rule of Christ. Why will there be any who would ever want war again? Sad to say, during the Millennium, some of the people on earth will only *pretend* to follow Christ. Even though they will have lived during the Millennium without war, murder, earthquake, famine, or serious disease, millions will openly turn against God. It is hard to believe. But the Bible is God's Word and it is true. How many will go to war on Satan's side? As many as "the grains of sand of the sea" (Revelation 20:7-9).

This huge army of Satan will surround Jerusalem and the people of God. But God in His great power will send fire from Heaven and destroy the whole army of unbelievers who will follow Satan. What a victory that will be!

Show Illustration #7

Then the devil will be thrown into the lake of fire which burns with sulphur. The Beast and the False Prophet will already be in the Lake of Fire (Revelation 19:20). There, the unholy trinity (Satan, Anti-Christ and the False Prophet) will be punished day and night forever. The devil will never, never be allowed to trick people again.

But what about all those people who never believed in Jesus Christ as Saviour and who will be in their graves? They will all be raised from the dead. But instead of being raised to everlasting joy, they will be raised for judgment.

4. THE GREAT WHITE THRONE JUDGMENT
Revelation 20:11-15

Show Illustration #8

The Judge of all the earth will be on the Great White Throne. And every unbelieving man, woman, teenager, boy and girl will be judged. All unsaved, great and small, old and young–indeed all unsaved who have been buried on land or drowned at sea–will be there! They will not get away from the throne of judgment.

Then the Lord will open some books. In the books are written all the works of every person–everything each one did on earth. Some are good deeds; but some are evil and wicked. In another book, a very special one called *the Book of Life*, are written the names of all those who have believed on Jesus Christ while living on earth.

One by one the names will be checked. But none of these will be listed in the Book of Life. Some did good deeds while on earth. But all their good deeds could never pay for their sins. Jesus Christ alone can pay the price for sins. And He did so when He died on the cross. When these people rejected Him, they refused God's way of salvation.

Each one whose name is not written in the Book of Life will be hurled into the lake of fire. This will be the second death, because they will then be separated from God for all eternity. How dreadful that will be: without God throughout eternity!

Eternity lasts forever and ever and ever. Do you know how long that is? Here in my hand I have a cup of sand.* How many grains of sand do you suppose are in this cup? You could guess, but I wouldn't be able to tell who would be right, for there are far too many for me to count.

I am going to take just one grain of sand, and I shall give it to you. (Indicate one of your students.) Suppose you start out and take this grain of sand to _____. (Name a distant city which your students know.) Of course, I want you to walk there. That would take quite a long time, wouldn't it? When you get there, go to the waterfront and leave this grain of sand. While you are there, pick up another grain and walk back here with it. When you get here, I shall put it in another cup and give you another grain out of this cup so you can do it all over again. I think you can easily understand that this could go on for a long time before you would have taken all this sand to the city.

I am trying to show you how long eternity is. For the time it would take you to empty this cup one grain at a time, is just this long (snap your fingers) in eternity. You will agree that it is certainly most important to know where you will be all during that time. The Bible says you will spend eternity either in Heaven or in hell, the lake of fire. It also explains how you can be sure it is Heaven. The Lord Jesus Christ said He would give eternal life to anyone who would believe in Him. Would you like to receive Him into your heart right now and be sure of spending all eternity in Heaven?

If you have previously done this, do you care about your friends and family who have not believed in the Lord Jesus? Do you pray for them? Do you live so all can see you are a true Christian and that you belong to God? Are you a faithful and bold witness for Him? If not, will you promise the Lord right now that, with His help, you will introduce Him to others this very week? Then, by receiving Christ as their Saviour from sin, they, too, can have the assurance of eternal life in Heaven.

*From *Easy Object Lessons,* by Dr. Charles C. Ryrie. Published by Moody Press, Chicago, IL, 60610. © 1970. Used by permission.

NOTE TO THE TEACHER

If you were to tell about the most beautiful city you had ever seen, how would you describe it? Would you tell of its buildings and gardens and parks? Or would you tell about the people in it? Both descriptions would be right. The New Jerusalem is described as to its walls, building materials and general appearance. It is also described as the bride, the Lamb's wife that is–the people who live in the city.

Do you, teacher, thrill at the thought of this glorious city yet to come? It will be the beginning of a new order. One Bible teacher describes it as: "A place of laughter without tears; of life without death; of content without crying; of singing without mourning; and of pleasure without pain." (G. Campbell Morgan)

Be faithful and hopeful, teacher. The best is yet to come!

Lesson 3
A NEW HEAVEN, A NEW EARTH, A NEW CITY

Scripture to be studied: Revelation 21

The *aim* of the lesson: To show that God will someday make all things new.

What your students should *know:* How entirely different the future will be when all sin is removed.

What your students should *feel:* A hatred for sin, and an anticipation of the glorious future.

What your students should *do:* Bow in sincere worship of the Lord.

Lesson outline (for the teacher's and students' notebooks):
1. The old passes away (Revelation 21:1).
2. The new appears (Revelation 21:2).
3. The glory of the city (Revelation 21:9-21).
4. The delights of the city (Revelation 21:22-27).

The verses to be memorized:

Alleluia: for the Lord God omnipotent reigneth. Let us be glad and rejoice and give honor to Him.
(Revelation 19:6b, 7a)

THE LESSON

Make-believe stories often end with the words, "And they lived happily ever after." But there is a true story which will end this way for multitudes of people. End? No, we must not say that, for there will be no end. It will go on and on and on forever. Would you like to be a part of this true story? Perhaps you are. Listen!

There was once a husband and wife who lived happily without tears or pain or sickness. They never had a thorn-prick, no upset stomach, no headache. They never experienced a dreary, stormy day. This couple loved each other dearly. They never hurt each other with an unkind word or deed.

Their home was a garden–never too cold, never too hot. All was perfect–perfect, until they turned for a moment from their obedience to God to one act of disobedience. Adam and Eve, the perfect couple, could have lived happily ever after if they had obeyed God. But they disobeyed. From that time on there have been tears, pain, sickness, death and unhappy homes. Oh, there may be some happy times. But there are also tears and sorrow.

If only there could be another opportunity to live happily ever after!

Good news! God is so loving and full of mercy that He has given the people of earth another opportunity. True, this whole earth has been scarred because of sin. But God sent His Son, Jesus Christ, so every person could be changed. Everyone who will turn from sin and believe in Jesus Christ as Saviour will receive everlasting life. With this new life comes the promise of everlasting joy. Someday then, each child of God will live happily ever after in a perfect place prepared by God. Until then, we live in a sinful world with storms and sorrow and sin.

1. THE OLD PASSES AWAY
Revelation 21:1

What I am going to tell you now may sound like a make-believe story. But it is not. It is absolutely true. It has not yet happened; but it *will* because God says so in His Word.

Long ago the Apostle John saw something almost unbelievable. In some future day there will be a new Heaven and a new earth. What will happen to the first Heaven and the first earth–the earth on which we are now living? They will be gone. They will pass away. Peter, a close friend of John, and also one of the twelve apostles, had already written that this very thing would happen.

Show Illustration #9

Peter wrote: "The heavens will pass away with a loud noise. Fire will melt it with great heat. The earth also and the works that are in it will be burned up." We can be sure that all who belong to God will be kept by Him in a safe place while the old earth and Heaven are burning with fire. Then Peter wrote, "But we are looking for what God promised–new heavens and a new earth in which righteousness lives." (See 2 Peter 3:4-14, especially verses 10 and 13.)

2. THE NEW APPEARS
Revelation 21:2

John speaks of this new place as a city. A huge city! A glowing city! A holy city!

Show Illustration #10

The city–called the New Jerusalem–will come down from God out of the new Heaven. It is a city which God will have ready.

In the future, when the city comes down, a great voice from Heaven will shout, "Look! The home of God is with all who have been saved. And He shall live with them. They will be His people. And God Himself will be among them. He will be their God."

In early Bible times there lived an old man, named Abraham. He was looking for a city which would be built by God. (See Hebrews 12:22-24; 11:8-16, especially verse 10.) He waited a long time but he has not seen that city even yet. Many people since Abraham have been waiting for that city to be ready.

The Apostles John and Peter heard the Lord Jesus promise, "I am going to prepare a place for you" (John 14:2-3). And John saw that there is to be a shining new city built by God. What will that city be like? It will be different from any place on earth. There will be no tears in that city, for God will wipe away every tear. Imagine–no more sorrow! No pain nor sickness! No headaches nor earaches! No colds nor flu, no measles, nor mumps, nor chicken pox! No leprosy nor cancer! No more germs! No death! No funerals!

God, sitting on His throne, told John, "Look! I am making all things new." And, "Write, because these words are true and faithful." Since they are true, they can be trusted and will surely come to pass.

Then God said, "I am the first and the last. I am the beginning and the end." No one was before God and God always will be. Jesus Christ always was and always will be.

God made three promises to those who are going to live in the new city. First, He said He will give complete satisfaction: "the water of life to anyone who is thirsty. It is a free gift." Second, He promised a full inheritance: "Those who truly believe will inherit (or receive) all things." His third promise is, "I will be his God and he will be My son"–perfect fellowship. What wonderful promises to those who will live in the Holy City!

Will any robbers get into that city? Of course not! Robbers will be in another place, the lake of fire. Listen carefully, for God tells exactly what kind of people will *not* be in that new and glorious city. The fearful (those who are afraid to believe in Jesus Christ as Saviour, afraid of what their friends might say) will not be in that city. Those who follow witchcraft, those who worship false gods, and all who keep on telling lies, will not be there. God Himself says: "They will have their part in the lake of fire and sulphur which is the second death." They will be separated from God forever.

3. THE GLORY OF THE CITY
Revelation 21:9-21

God gave John (in the long ago) a close-up view of the New Jerusalem. And from his writing we learn that it will be a city filled with the glory of God; filled with the fulness of God Himself. It will shine brighter than light, like a rich jewel, clear as crystal. There will be a high wall around the city. (The wall reminds us that all who are inside that city will be safe forever.) There will be twelve (12) gates, three (3) gates in the east wall, three gates in the north wall, three in the south and three in the west wall. (See Illustration #10.) At each gate there will be an angel. There will be twelve names written, one on each gate. These will be the names of the twelve tribes of Israel. God promised He would never forget the people He chose for Himself. And He will keep His promise!

The wall will have twelve foundation stones. The names of the twelve apostles of Christ will be on the stones. The apostles remind us of the Church, the body of Christ. God will never forget His Church–all His people who have placed their trust in Christ.

Show Illustration #11

The angel who talked to John had a golden stick in his hand. With it he measured the city, the gates and the wall. He discovered that the new, holy city will be perfectly square. It will be about 1,500 miles long, 1,500 miles wide and 1,500 miles high. Can you imagine such a gigantic city? How large is that? (*Teacher:* Indicate an area with which your students are acquainted. It will be about half as large as the United States. In Europe, it will be equal in size to all of England, Ireland, France, Spain, Italy, Germany, Austria,

Greece and Turkey. The city will be larger than all of India.) Only God could make such a city!

We have no way of knowing *exactly* how God's new city will look. But it will be bigger and better by far than anything man has ever made.

The city itself will be made of pure gold like clear glass. Can you imagine looking right through the clear gold? What a city!

The 12 gates in the walls will be 12 gigantic pearls. Each gate will be one pearl–a pearl large enough to be a gate! God alone could make such pearls. Do you know how a pearl is formed? Pearls come from oysters in the ocean. When a tiny bit of sand gets inside the oyster, it hurts. So the oyster forms a pearl around that irritating piece of sand. The true Church is sometimes spoken of as "the pearl of great price." Jesus Christ suffered so that the pearl, the Church of Jesus Christ, might be formed. (See Matthew 13:45-46; Ephesians 5:25-27.)

So the 12 gates will be reminders forever of Christ's suffering for His Church. Think of it! The Lord Jesus suffered for you and for me that we might live happily ever after with Him.

The streets of the new city will be made of pure gold, as clear as glass. How would you like to walk on those streets some day?

4. THE DELIGHTS OF THE CITY
Revelation 21:22-27

John could see inside the golden city, but he could not see a temple anywhere. Why? Because the presence of God Almighty and the Lamb of God *are* the temple. There will be no need to offer sacrifices for sin; for there will be no more sin, no need for cleansing.

The city will not need the light of the sun or moon. The glory of God will fill the city with light. And the Lamb of God will be the lamp of the city. God the Father and God the Son will fill the city with great brightness.

Show Illustration #12

Only those whose names are written in the Lamb's Book of Life will be there.

Is your name written in the Lamb's Book of Life? It is if you have placed all your trust in Christ the Lord. Are you living to please the Lord, your Saviour? Are you looking forward with joy to being with Him forever? Remember! Because of what the Lord Jesus did, those who have trusted in Him can live happily with Him and with God forever.

Let us bow and worship and say, "Alleluia: for the Lord God omnipotent reigneth. Let us be glad and rejoice and give honor to Him" (Revelation 19:6b-7a).

> **NOTE TO THE TEACHER**
> Allow time for the students to really worship God and to express their worship in their own words.

Lesson 4
ETERNITY WITH GOD

Scripture to be studied: Revelation 22

The *aim* of the lesson: To show that Jesus Christ may come at any time.

  What your students should *know*: That many will not be ready when Jesus Christ comes.

  What your students should *feel*: A desire to be prepared for His coming. Also, to be concerned for those who are not ready.

  What your students should *do*: Expect the coming of the Lord Jesus at any time. Be pure and ready. Show others the way to be ready (by their lives and words).

Lesson outline (for the teacher's and students' notebooks):
1. The river and the tree (Revelation 22:1-2).
2. Six more wonders (Revelation 22:3-5).
3. Faithful and true words (Revelation 22:6-16).
4. Last message and last warning (Revelation 22:17-21).

The verses to be memorized:

Alleluia: for the Lord God omnipotent reigneth. Let us be glad and rejoice and give honor to Him.

(Revelation 19:6b, 7a)

THE LESSON

Mary Ellen was 12 years old. She had been blind since she was born. Although she was almost a teenager she had never seen a bird, a flower, or a tree. She could never enjoy the beauty of nature. Often Mary Ellen's mother would tell her about the red and yellow flowers, the green grass, the giant trees, the

> **NOTE TO THE TEACHER**
> Revelation 21 and 22 refer to Genesis 1 and 2. There we have the record of Paradise lost. And in Revelation, the prophecy of Paradise regained. Revelation was given by God for a definite purpose. It was written to be read and heard (Revelation 1:3). But how many have read or heard it? It was written to teach and to warn. How many have heard the teachings and warnings? Thank you, teacher, for doing your part. All who heed the truths taught are promised blessing. Surely you have been blessed and will be blessed as you faithfully teach the lessons from this revealing book.
>
> On Illustration #16, print Christ's words: "I am coming quickly." On Illustration #17, print "Come, Lord Jesus."

birds flying through the air, the many-colored sunsets. "Tell me again," her daughter would plead.

Her parents were concerned. Often they said, "If only Mary Ellen could see!" One day they heard of a doctor who had been successful with eye operations. They took their daughter to him to be examined. Could he do something to help the blind girl?

The doctor decided to operate on Mary Ellen. Finally, days later, the bandages were taken off. The girl blinked. She jumped from the bed and ran to the window. She saw the soft green grass for the first time, the colorful flowers, the blossoming trees, the blue sky. Turning to her mother, she asked, "Why didn't you tell me it was so beautiful?"

Her mother answered, "I tried. But I couldn't."

The Apostle John has written an amazing description of the New Jerusalem–the beautiful eternal, heavenly city. He tells of God's glorious throne, the golden streets, the jasper walls, the gates of pearl. Everything will be magnificent beyond words. We try to picture it in our minds. But it is impossible to imagine exactly what the heavenly city will be like.

In the last chapter of Revelation (which is the last chapter of the entire Bible), John again described more wonders of that new place which God will have ready for His own.

1. THE RIVER AND THE TREE
Revelation 22:1-2

The angel showed John a river of the water of life. It will sparkle like clear crystal and be pure as all of Heaven. The river is a reminder that everyone in the city will have lives full of continual blessings.

Show Illustration #13

The crystal river will flow from the throne of God. This throne will be occupied by God the Father and God the Son. (See 1 Corinthians 15:24-28.) The holy city will have golden streets. In the middle of it and on each side of the river there will be the tree of life. (*Teacher:* The tree of life is believed to be a particular kind of tree, not necessarily one single tree since it is said to be on both sides of the river.)

We have heard before of the tree of life. Adam and Eve could have eaten of this tree in the Garden of Eden. After they sinned they were sent out of the garden. An angel with a sword guarded the garden. So Adam and Eve could not get back into it. Neither could they eat of the tree of life. Do you know why? If they had eaten of the tree of life after they sinned, Adam and Eve would have lived forever as sinners.

So the tree of life with 12 different kinds of fruit will grow in the heavenly city, the New Jerusalem.

2. SIX MORE WONDERS
Revelation 22:3-5

There will be six more wonders in the new, eternal city.

First, there will be no more curse. All the harmful and unhappy things of earth will be gone. There will be no more violent storms. No weeds. No poor soil. No plant disease. No harmful insects or dangerous animals. And–most important–no sin at all.

Show Illustration #14

Second, God's people will serve Him. There are some who think the people of God will float on clouds and play harps for all eternity. Not so. God's people will worship Him and serve Him. They will always please Him. They will never make a mistake, nor get tired.

The third wonder is that all the redeemed (saved) will look on the face of the Lord Jesus. Those who belong to the family of God shall see Christ in all His glory and majesty. On earth His heavenly glory was not seen. But in Heaven believers shall see Him as He really is. Those who belong to Him will adore Him and praise Him who loved us and died for us.

A person's face shows what he/she is like. When the Lord Jesus was on earth He said to God in prayer: "Father, I want those whom You have given to Me (all believers) to be with Me where I am; that they may see My glory which You gave Me" (John 17:24). When those who belong to Him see His face, they will see His shining glory.

Listen to this fourth wonder: The name of God will be on the foreheads of those who belong to Him. The number 666 will be on the foreheads and hands of unbelievers during the Tribulation. But in eternity those who have trusted in the Lord will have His name on their foreheads. (See Revelation 3:12.) They will belong to God, and God will belong to them forever.

The fifth wonder is something mentioned before in the book of Revelation. There will be no night in that heavenly city–no darkness at all! No lamp, no candle, nor even the sun will be needed. Why? Because the Lord God is the light. Heaven will be bright all the time. Can you imagine a light so bright that it lights up the whole city 1,500 miles long, 1,500 miles wide and 1,500 miles high? God is light. In that day when all sin is removed, His light will shine everywhere.

The sixth wonder is this: His servants will reign (or rule) with Him. If you were chosen here on earth to rule with a king (or president), would you be honored? Think of reigning with Christ! It is the highest privilege to *serve* the Lord. But imagine the thrill of *ruling* with Him! How amazing and generous of God to let His own share in that blessing! (See 2 Timothy 2:12; also Revelation 3:21.) Everyone who will be ruling with the Lord will have the wisdom and power which God will give. Remember! Only those who have received Christ as Saviour here on earth and are faithful to Him, will reign with Him in eternity.

3. FAITHFUL AND TRUE WORDS
Revelation 22:6-16

The prophecies and warnings of judgment have been written in Revelation for all to read. Yet some have laughed at these words. Many refuse to believe them. But an angel of God said: "These words are faithful and true." In His Book, the Lord has given the order of events which could begin to happen at any time–whenever God gives the signal. (See Revelation 22:6.) Since what God says is true, we must believe His Word and tell others what He has said.

The Apostle John heard the Lord Jesus say, "I am coming quickly." Perhaps you say, "Jesus made that promise almost 2,000 years ago. But He has not come. Why?"

The word "quickly" can mean *suddenly* or *at any time*. And this is how Jesus is going to come. He will come all suddenly, when some are not expecting Him. God's timing is different from the way we think of time. (See 2 Peter 3:8-10; compare Romans 13:11.) "One day is with the Lord as a thousand years, and a thousand years as one day." If we think of time in God's way, then 2,000 years is only two days. And two days pass quickly.

Show Illustration #15

The Lord Jesus Christ is coming. Before the seven years of awful tribulation and the 1,000 glorious years of His reign on earth, Jesus will come in the clouds. He will snatch His own and take them up to be with Him forever. (This is the *Rapture*.) We are *much* closer to His coming today than John was when he heard the words "Jesus Christ is coming." Are you glad the Lord is coming? Are you ready?

God wrote (through John): "Happy is the one who keeps [obeys] the words of the prophecy of this book." If you are not happy, perhaps you are not obeying these words. Perhaps you are not looking for the Lord Jesus to come at any moment.

God says that when Christ comes, people will not change. The unjust and sinful will remain that way forever. The righteous and the holy will continue to be righteous. So now is the time to change to God's way. Some day it will be too late.

Christ's words, "I am coming quickly," were repeated as a reminder to everyone to be ready at all times. Jesus also said, "I am bringing My reward with Me to repay everyone according to his deeds." A person's good deeds will not get him into Heaven. But a believer's good deeds, done after he is saved, will be repaid by God. (See 1 Corinthians 3:11-15.) Are you faithful in serving the Lord now?

Do not miss this promise of Revelation: "Happy are those who wash their robes [by the blood of the Lamb]. They may enter through the gates of the city. They will have the right to eat of the fruit of the tree of life." Have you the clean garments of salvation, purified by the precious blood of Jesus Christ?

John listened carefully as the Lord Jesus spoke: "I, Jesus, have sent My angel to tell you these things in the churches. I am the root and offspring of David." Jesus Christ, God the Son, was David's Creator and Lord. Yet Jesus Christ was born from the family of David. He became truly human, but remained truly God also! And He will fulfill all these promises to the people of Israel as well as to all believers.

The Lord also said, "I am the bright and morning star." The morning star is the bright star seen in the sky early in the morning. It tells us that the day is almost here. Jesus Christ is coming, and it may be soon. The night of sin and darkness will then be over. Are you watching and waiting and working for Him?

4. LAST MESSAGE AND WARNING
Revelation 22:17-21

While we are still waiting for the Lord Jesus Christ to come, the last great invitation is given to all. The Holy Spirit and the bride of Jesus Christ say, "Come." Come to the Lord Jesus, turn from your sin and receive eternal salvation. It is a free gift. How can anyone resist such a loving invitation? Do not wait. Come to Jesus right now and you will have everlasting life.

The very last warning in the Bible was given for men and women and boys and girls of all nations and of all time. Listen to it carefully: "I am telling this to everyone who hears the words of the prophecy of this book. If anyone adds anything to what is written in this book, God will add to him the kinds of trouble that this book tells about. If anyone takes away from the words of the book of this prophecy, God will take away his part from the tree of life and from the Holy City and from the things which are written in this book."

What a warning! The prophecies found in the book of Revelation are true. God's Word is final.

Show Illustration #16

Finally the Lord Jesus Christ repeated for the third time in this chapter: "Surely I am coming quickly." And John answered, "Even so, come, Lord Jesus."

Revelation closes the Bible with these beautiful words, "The grace of our Lord Jesus Christ be with you all. Amen [So be it]."

It is only by God's grace that anyone will live with Jesus Christ forever. No one deserves such honor. But God's Son offers you Himself and all of eternity with Him forever. If you have not come to Him, will you do so now? If you believe Christ is the Son of God, will you receive Him as your Saviour? If you have already come, will you promise to serve Him faithfully, looking for His sure return?

Show Illustration #17

Can you say, "COME, LORD JESUS!"?

The King's Timeline

The Tribulation
7 Years
(Rev. 4:1-19:10)

The Millenium
1,000 Years
(Rev. 19:19-20:15)

Eternity
Forever
(Rev. 21:1-22:21)

The next event in God's calendar
(1 Thessalonians 4:13-17; 1 Corinthians 15:51-52, date unknown)

On earth:

7 Scroll Judgments (Rev. 6:1-17)
1. False peace
2. War
3. Famine
4. Death
5. Martyrs
6. Earthquake
7. Sun, moon, stars affected

7 Trumpet Judgments (Rev. 8:1-9:21; 11:15-19)
1. Grass and 1/3 of trees destroyed by fire
2. 1/3 of sea becomes blood; 1/3 of sea life dies; 1/3 of ships destroyed
3. 1/3 of rivers poisoned
4. Sun, moon and stars darkened
5. Demons torment people
6. 1/3 of people killed (Two witnesses murdered, resurrected and ascend to Heaven (Revelation 11:3-12)
7. Earthquake

7 Bowl Judgments (Rev. 16:1-12, 17-21)
1. Painful sores on those who have the mark of the Anti-Christ
2. Sea turns to blood; everything in the sea dies
3. Rivers turn to blood
4. People burned by sun
5. Anti-Christ's kingdom darkened; people gnaw their tongues because of pain
6. Euphrates River dries up
7. Earthquake; cities, islands, mountains disappear

In Heaven:

At the middle of the Tribulation:
1. Satan and his angels fight against the angels of God
2. Satan and his angels hurled out of Heaven down to earth (Rev. 12:7-10)
3. Satan comes to earth with fury, knowing his time is short (Rev. 12:12)

At the end of the Tribulation:
The wedding of Christ and the Church (Rev. 19:1-10)

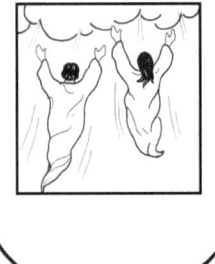

At the beginning:
(Rev. 19:11-20:6)

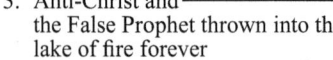

1. Christ returns to earth, bringing His own with Him
2. Christ defeats Satan's army at Armageddon
3. Anti-Christ and the False Prophet thrown into the lake of fire forever
4. Satan chained in the abyss for 1,000 years
5. Christ reigns as King on the earth for 1,000 years

At the end: (Rev. 20:7-10)

1. Satan freed from the abyss for a short time
2. Satan and his followers fight against God's people in Jerusalem
3. God sends fire from Heaven and destroys Satan's followers
4. Satan hurled into the lake of fire forever

After the Millenium ends:
(Rev. 20:11-21:8)

1. Heavens and earth burned with fire
2. The Great White Throne Judgment
3. Unbelievers cast into the lake of fire forever
4. Believers of all ages spend eternity in New Jerusalem in God's presence

New Heavens and New Earth

The heavenly city (the holy Jerusalem)

The eternal home of all who trust in Christ

While teaching the four lessons in this volume, continually refer your students to the events on this chart. Encourage them to copy the complete chart in their notebooks.

During the Tribulation on Earth

Multitudes from all over the world (who never before heard the Gospel) will be saved–including 144,000 Jews.

The 144,000 saved Jews will be protected by God from Satan.

© Bible Visuals International, Inc

www.ingramcontent.com/pod-product-compliance
Lightning Source LLC
Chambersburg PA
CBHW060801090426
42736CB00002B/113